A SPECTACULAR SEEK AND FIND CHALLENGE FOR ALL AGES!

BIGFOOT™

SPOTTED AT WORLD-FAMOUS LANDMARKS

D. L. MILLER

Happy Fox
BOOKS™

For Mom and Dad, and the Miller brothers who grew up in our little house nestled in the mountains of Western Maryland, where we spent many a day exploring the beauty and mysteries of the woods and creek bottoms just outside our front door.

— D. L. Miller

A Big Thank You

to all the BigFoot hunters around the world who not only believe that our big furry friend really does exist, but more importantly that he continues to inspire us to go outside and explore this great big world.

A Special Thank You

to the wonderful folks at Fox Chapel Publishing for bringing the BigFoot Seek and Find series to life, especially…

Publisher: Alan Giagnocavo
Vice President – Content: Christopher Reggio
Senior Editor: Laura Taylor
Managing Editor: Melissa Younger
Contributing Editors: Anthony Regolino, Jeremy Hauck, Katie Ocasio
Graphic Designer: David Fisk

© 2018 by D. L. Miller and Happy Fox Books, an imprint of Fox Chapel Publishing Company, Inc., 903 Square Street, Mount Joy, PA 17552.

Bigfoot Spotted at World-Famous Landmarks is an original work, first published in 2018 by Fox Chapel Publishing Company, Inc.

ISBN 978-1-64124-002-4

Library of Congress Cataloging-in-Publication Data

Names: Miller, D. L. (David Lee), 1965- author, illustrator.
Title: BigFoot spotted at world-famous landmarks / D.L. Miller.
Description: Mount Joy, Pennsylvania : Happy Fox Books, an imprint of Fox Chapel Publishing Company, Inc., 2018. | Audience: Ages: 5-12.
Identifiers: LCCN 2018015224 | ISBN 9781641240024 (hardcover)
Subjects: LCSH: Sasquatch--Juvenile literature. | Geography--Juvenile literature.
Classification: LCC QL89.2.S2 M576 2018 | DDC 001.944--dc23
LC record available at https://lccn.loc.gov/2018015224

To learn more about the other great books from Fox Chapel Publishing, or to find a retailer near you, call toll-free 800-457-9112 or visit us at *www.FoxChapelPublishing.com*.

We are always looking for talented authors. To submit an idea, please send a brief inquiry to acquisitions@foxchapelpublishing.com.

Fox Chapel Publishing makes every effort to use environmentally friendly paper for printing.

Printed in China
First printing

Shutterstock images: Adwo (35 bottom left); Aleksandr Pobedimskiy (15 middle left & bottom center); Alessandro Colle (11 bottom right foreground); Alessio Catelli (27 bottom right); AlexanderZam (26 middle); Alfonso de Tomas (27 middle center); Alistair McDonald (38 top left); Al Mueller (42 bottom center); Aneese (35 top right); apezfauzy (7 top center); aphotostory (19 top right); a_v_d (18 middle right); AxelMezini (14 bottom); Benny Marty (22 bottom left, 39 bottom left); Beth Ruggiero-York (35 bottom center); Bill Perry (27 middle left); Bradley Blackburn (39 bottom right); Bryan Busovicki (34 bottom background); caamalf (23 top left); Catarina Belova (30 bottom); chuyuss (19 bottom left); critterbiz (42 top right); Dan Kaplan (43 middle right); Dan Thornberg (top right); Dejan Dajkovic (23 middle/bottom left); Dmitrii_Miki (22 top right); Dmitry Finkel (19 middle right); Dorothy Puray-Isidro (6 bottom); Elnur (14 top right); eurobanks (42 bottom left); Everett Historical (22 bottom right; 34 bottom right); Fedor Selivanov (7 middle); Felix Lipov (23 top right); Gearstd (42 middle left); Glevalex (43 middle left); GTS Productions (7 top left); Gurgen Bakhshetyan (27 top right); Igor Filonenko (35 bottom left); Igorsky (31 middle/bottom right); igorstevanovic (39 top right); iku4 (31 bottom right); James A. Harris (42 middle right); James Kirkikis (23 bottom center); Janaka Dharmasena (38 middle left); John Lock (18 bottom left; 19 middle left); Laborant (7 top right); leodaphne (38 top right); lolya1988 (6 top left; 10 top left; 14 top left; 18 top left; 22 top left; 26 top left; 30 top left; 34 top left; 38 top left; 42 top left); Luciano Mortula – LGM (10 bottom right); Luis Louro (31 bottom left); Lynn Y (34 middle); Mikhail Kolesnikov (11 middle right); Min C. Chiu (11 top); musicalryo (15 middle right); NaughtyNut (43 middle center); Netfalls Remy Musser (26 bottom left); oksana.perkins (35 bottom right); Oliver Hitchen (31 top center); Paolo Trovo (34 top right); Parmna (15 bottom left); Pascale Gueret (11 bottom left foreground); Paul Juser (5 top right); Pecold (15 bottom right); pisaphotography (22 middle right); PRILL (19 top left, bottom right); Prin Adulyatham (6 top right); prochasson Frederic (11 middle left); Pung (10 bottom center); Rashevskyi Viacheslav (19 middle center); Richard Peterson (39 middle); RomanYa (38 bottom left); Rudy Riva (4 bottom); Sharon Keating (4 middle center); SherSS (15 top right); shootmybusiness (14 middle); showcake (42 top center, middle center; 43 top right, middle center, bottom left); SnappixPro (31 background); somchaij (11 bottom right background); Stanislav Fosenbauer (38 bottom); Steve Allen (39 middle/bottom left); superjoseph (18 bottom center); TheBlackRhino (18 middle left, middle center, middle right); TTstudio (26 top right); Utir (5 bottom); vectorOK (38 top right); Vern Faber (43 bottom right); Viacheslav Lopatin (27 middle right, bottom left; 30 top); Vlad G (26 bottom right); volkova natalia (31 middle center); WitthayaP (7 bottom left); Wuttichok Panichiwarapun (7 background, 8 background, 9 background)

BiGFOOT CONTENTS

Travel the world with BigFoot as he discovers some of the coolest structures and wildest geography on our planet!

HOW TO USE THiS BOOK

Read a bit about each landmark.
You may learn something surprising!

Turn the page and search for BigFoot. The keys along the sides tell you what else to look for. Good luck!

WHO IS BIGFOOT?

Stories about BigFoot have been around for years all over the world. Some people believe he's a **giant bear** that walks around on two legs. Others think he may be a **giant gorilla** roaming the forests.

This picture is from the famous **Patterson-Gimlin film**, taken in 1967 in Northern California's **Six Rivers National Forest** by Roger Patterson and Bob Gimlin. Some people think this is just a person in a costume. Others believe it's the real **BigFoot**. What do you think?

BIG FOOT XING

DUE TO SIGHTINGS IN THE AREA OF A CREATURE RESEMBLING "BIG FOOT" THIS SIGN HAS BEEN POSTED FOR YOUR SAFETY

HAVE YOU SEEN A REAL BIGFOOT?

BigFoot is believed to be a large, furry creature standing **7 feet (2.3 m) to 9 feet (3 m) tall**. BigFoot is brown, although many have also reported seeing black, gray, white, and greenish-blue BigFoots. Some people think he has **large eyes** and a large forehead. The top of his head is said to be like the shape of a large gorilla. If you see someone walking around that looks like this, you're probably looking at BigFoot!

It's been reported that BigFoot can run up to 30 miles per hour (48 kph)—a person can only run half that speed!

WHERE DID THE NAME *BIGFOOT* COME FROM?

In the 1800s, the name *BigFoot* was used for huge **grizzly bears** that were seen in parts of the United States. Some believe that **David Thompson**, a man crossing the Rocky Mountains in the winter of 1811, found the first real BigFoot footprints in the snow. The tracks were too big for even the **largest bear**. The name was again used when people started spotting **huge footprints** in the forest that looked bigger than a bear's. These footprints were about 24 inches (61 cm) long and 8 inches (20 cm) wide, **twice as big** as an adult shoe. Many people believe that these big footprints are enough proof that our BigFoot **really does exist!**

BiGFOOT GOES BY MANY NAMES

BigFoot has many names around the world, including the most common: **Sasquatch**. So don't forget to tell people you're going **"Squatching"** the next time you decide to search for our giant, furry friend. What do other parts of the world call BigFoot?

Barmanou (Pakistan)

Basajuan (Spain)

Big Greyman (Scotland)

Gin-Sung (China)

Hibagon (Japan)

Kapre (Philippines)

Kushtaka (Alaska, USA)

Mapinguari (Brazil and Bolivia)

Menk (Russia)

Moehau (New Zealand)

Mogollon Monster (Arizona, USA)

Orange Pendek (Indonesia)

Skunk Ape (Florida, USA)

Ucu (Argentina)

Waterbobbejaan (South Africa)

Wendigo (Canada)

Woodwosa (England)

Yeren (Mongolia)

Yeti (Russia)

Yowie (Australia)

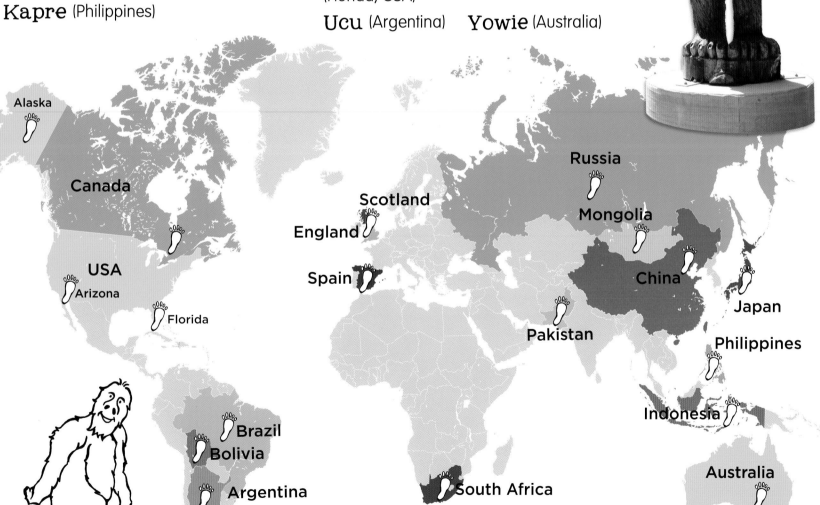

5

Pyramids of Giza

A pyramid is a huge tomb where a pharaoh (ruler of ancient Egypt) was buried.

ANCIENT WONDERS

In **Giza**, Egypt, the pyramids are on the west side of the Nile River. They were built between 2584 and 2490 BCE—over **4,500** years ago! There are three main pyramids. There are also smaller pyramids for the pharaohs' family, **temples**, the **Sphinx**, and a town where the pyramid builders lived.

The average weight of each block is about 2.5 tons (2.3 metric tons)—the same weight as a full-grown giraffe or rhinoceros.

Mau cats are one of the oldest kinds of cats. "Mau" is Egyptian for "cat."

GREAT PYRAMID

The Great Pyramid is the oldest and biggest of the pyramids. It was built as the tomb for **Khufu**, a pharaoh who ruled from about 2589 BCE to about 2566 BCE. Each side of the pyramid's base is **751** feet (229 m) long. In all, it covers 13 acres (5 ha) and weighs 6.5 million tons. It took 2,300,000 blocks of limestone and granite to build this greatest Great Pyramid!

VIC: VERY IMPORTANT CAT

Ancient Egyptians worshipped gods and goddesses who were supposed to help and protect them. The goddess Bastet was imagined as a cat-woman. She was supposed to protect homes and children, just as real cats protected their human families by killing snakes and scorpions. The Egyptians made cats their special pets. They treated them as family and were even buried with them.

PICTURE LANGUAGE

Many of the pyramids' walls are covered with ancient Egyptian writing that used a hieroglyphic—or picture—alphabet. The pictures show ideas or a group of sounds to make words.

SPHINX

A sphinx is a pretend creature that has a lion's body and a human's head. Built over 4,000 years ago, the Sphinx statue at Giza is believed to show Pharaoh Khafre's face. It was built to guard the pyramid tombs. It measures 65 feet (20 m) high, 241 feet (74 m) long, and 20 feet (6 m) wide. It was carved by hand from limestone, making it the biggest and oldest statue on Earth.

SHIPS OF THE DESERT

Arabian camels, also called dromedaries, live in northern Africa. They have been carrying people and supplies over long distances for thousands of years. They have one hump where they store fat that they can use for energy. A camel can live for a week or more without water. A thirsty camel can slurp 30 gallons (114 l) of water in 13 minutes!

BEAUTIFUL BEETLES

Scarab beetles meant eternal life and rebirth. Why? Scarab beetles lay their eggs inside animal dung. Then they shape the dung into a ball, rolling it wherever the beetle wants to go. When the eggs hatched, Egyptians thought the baby beetles appeared magically—as if the scarab beetle could instantly create life. Ancient Egyptians wore scarab beetle–shaped jewelry (called amulets) to protect them from harm.

1 BigFoot

1 Legendary Footprint

11 Gliding Egyptian Vultures

6 Royal Jackals

10 White Scarab Beetles

4 Camels with Keepers

7 Mau Cats with Gold Collars

5 Talkative Tour Guides

2 Egyptian Gold Masks

Golden Gate Bridge

BUT IT'S NOT GOLDEN!

This orange bridge is named for the **Golden Gate Strait** that it crosses—not for a color. The strait is the entrance into the San Francisco Bay from the Pacific Ocean. It was named in 1846 by **John C. Fremont** because it was a "**golden**," or perfect, way to sail to countries across the Pacific Ocean.

Corrosion is when metal is weakened and worn away.

WHY ORANGE?

"International Orange" was used so ships coming into San Francisco Bay and planes flying by could easily see the bridge, even on a foggy night.

See if you can find BigFoot when he visited San Francisco! Check out *BigFoot Visits the Big Cities of the World*.

ALWAYS PAINTING

Parts of the bridge are always being repainted. **Painting** the bridge's steel cables and towers protects it from the salt in the air that can cause **corrosion**. There are **34 brave painters** who climb all over the bridge to keep it safe and strong—and beautiful!

Over 110,000 cars and trucks cross the bridge each day!

It costs $7.75 for a car to cross the bridge.

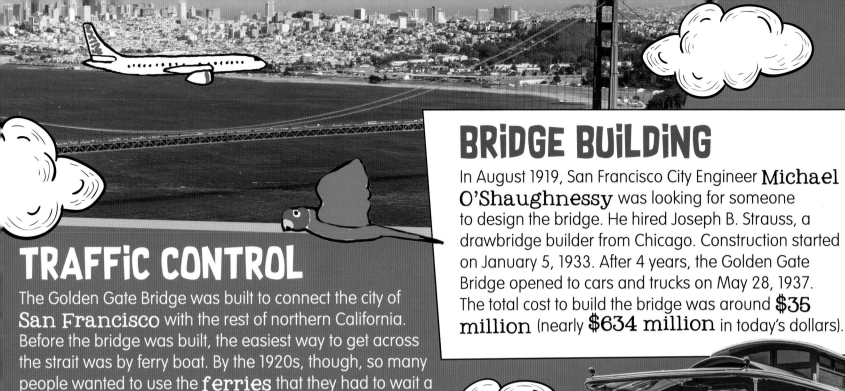

BRIDGE BUILDING

In August 1919, San Francisco City Engineer **Michael O'Shaughnessy** was looking for someone to design the bridge. He hired Joseph B. Strauss, a drawbridge builder from Chicago. Construction started on January 5, 1933. After 4 years, the Golden Gate Bridge opened to cars and trucks on May 28, 1937. The total cost to build the bridge was around **$35 million** (nearly **$634 million** in today's dollars).

TRAFFIC CONTROL

The Golden Gate Bridge was built to connect the city of **San Francisco** with the rest of northern California. Before the bridge was built, the easiest way to get across the strait was by ferry boat. By the 1920s, though, so many people wanted to use the **ferries** that they had to wait a long time to sail across. There had to be a better way!

BRIDGE STATS

The Golden Gate Bridge is a **suspension** bridge: a tall tower is at each end, and two huge metal cables connect them. Each one is 7,650 feet (2,332 m) long. These cables are **super strong**, since each one is made of **27,572 wires**. The total length of wire used in both cables is 80,000 miles (129,000 km). This is almost the distance of going around the Earth **3 times**! There are also 250 pairs of vertical suspension cables holding the road in place. The road is about 220 feet (67 m) above the water.

Suspension bridges move! The road is connected to cables that can move a little. So the road will move, too, when there's strong wind or if there's a lot of weight on it.

Blue whales, gray whales, and humpback whales have all been seen in the San Francisco Bay.

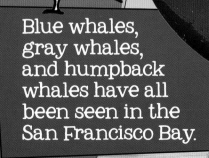

BiGFOOT
VISITS THE GOLDEN GATE BRIDGE

1 BigFoot

1 Legendary Footprint

11 Green Gliding Sailboats

5 Pelicans with Yellow Beaks

5 Coyotes on the Move

7 Bold and Brave Bridge Painters

4 Happy Jumping Whales

6 Floating Red Buoys

11 Silly Sea Lions

Stonehenge

ROCK ON

In a field near **Salisbury, England**, there is a strange man-made circle of standing stones called Stonehenge. **Archaeologists** believe ancient people began building Stonehenge 5,000 years ago. But they're not sure why they did! It took them over **1,000 years** to build the monument.

? A HARD QUESTION ?

There are **83 stones** in this famous monument. Some of them weigh up to **4 tons** (3,600 kg)—the weight of **two cars**! The tallest of them reaches 30 feet (9 m). Some of the stones are a kind of sandstone called **sarsen** that came from a quarry 25 miles (40 km) away. The inner ring of **bluestones** came from Wales, a country 170 miles (274 km) away. How could ancient people move and stand up such heavy stones?

BIGFOOT
A SPECTACULAR SEEK AND FIND CHALLENGE FOR ALL AGES!
Visits the Big Cities of the World

London is only a 2-hour drive from Stonehenge! Can you spot BigFoot there in *BigFoot Visits the Big Cities of the World*?

More than 1,000,000 tourists visit Stonehenge each year!

STONE MOVERS

Archaeologists think ancient people put the **sarsen stones** on big wooden sleds and dragged them to the site. The **bluestones** may have been dragged on strong wooden sleds to a **river** and then placed on sturdy rafts to float to the site.

Sarsen stones are sandstone boulders found in southern England.

Until the 1500s, people thought that the wizard Merlin magically moved the heavy stones from Ireland to where they are today in England.

BUILDING FACTS

Before raising the stones, the builders shaped them with stone **chisels** and **hammers**. They made them fit together like a puzzle. Next, deep ditches were dug by the bottom of each stone. Then, using **ropes**, strong wooden **poles**, and a lot of **muscle** power, the stones were raised. The ditches were filled with rocks and dirt so the stones wouldn't move.

GUESSES AND THEORIES

No one knows for sure what **Stonehenge** was used for. A kind of calendar for studying the stars? A temple to worship sun or **moon gods**? Or a place that could give magical healing? One of its uses may have been a **cemetery**, since archaeologists have found the bones of ancient people there.

A quarry is an open pit where people dig out stone, slate, or limestone.

1 BigFoot

1 Legendary Footprint

5 Selfie-Taking Tourists

3 Chatty Tour Guides

6 Rattling Ravens

5 Eager English Sheepdogs

6 Pondering Tourists Looking Up

10 Sleepy Sheep

3 On-Guard Herding Dogs

Great Wall of China

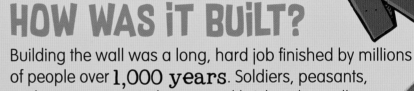

You can visit the Great Wall today. Go in the spring or autumn to avoid summer's heat and crowds, and winter's cold.

WALL OF DEFENSE

When the Great Wall of China was first being built over **2,000 years ago**, it wasn't just one wall. There were lots of walls made by fighting **dynasties** (ruling families). In 220 BCE, Emperor **Qin Shi Huang** united the people of China. He ordered that the walls connect to one another. The single wall was built to keep out invaders like the **Mongols**. He had guard towers built along the wall for soldiers to defend his empire.

HOW WAS IT BUILT?

Building the wall was a long, hard job finished by millions of people over **1,000 years**. Soldiers, peasants, and prisoners carried stone and brick to the wall. Sometimes they even carried it up a mountain. The workers lined up in **human chains** to pass everything to the builders. In flat areas, the workers used **wheelbarrows** or used horses and oxen to pull carts.

Not far from the Great Wall is the Forbidden City, where you can search for BigFoot and cool penjing trees (*BigFoot Visits the Big Cities of the World*).

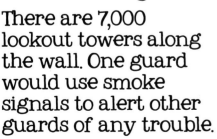

There are 7,000 lookout towers along the wall. One guard would use smoke signals to alert other guards of any trouble.

THE MING DYNASTY

The Great Wall was more like a really long fortress during the **Ming Dynasty** in the 1400s. When Emperor **Yongle** moved the capital to **Beijing**, the wall was very important for defending China. The wall was made stronger with **more bricks**. Most of the wall we see today is due to the major work done during the Ming dynasty.

The wall is the longest man-made structure on Earth!

It is a myth that the Great Wall of China can be seen from space.

The wall is about 5,500 miles (8,851 km) long and runs along part of the northern border of China.

GREAT ANIMALS OF CHINA

You'll find more than people at the Great Wall. There are wild boars, pheasants, red foxes, snakes, and deer living near the wall. As you travel through China, you'll also find giant pandas, golden monkeys, Siberian tigers, cranes, red pandas, and yaks.

BiGFOOT
VISITS THE GREAT WALL OF CHINA

1 BigFoot

1 Legendary Footprint

5 Red Pandas

5 Baby Tigers

5 Chinese Golden Monkeys

14 Great Cormorants

3 Delightful Dragons

5 Giant Pandas

5 Giant Chinese Salamanders

Statue of Liberty

SYMBOL OF FREEDOM

The famous statue, whose full name is "Liberty Enlightening the World," is on Liberty Island in New York Harbor. Between 1886 and 1924, **14 million people** sailed past this statue. They came to America from England, Ireland, Germany, and other parts of Europe. Lady Liberty welcomed **immigrants** to a land of hope and freedom.

An immigrant is someone who goes to a country to live there.

AS TALL AS A 30-STORY BUILDING

Weighing in at **225** tons, the statue is about 151 feet (46 m) from the base to the tip of the torch. It is a little over **305 feet** (93 m) if you include the pedestal. BigFoot will have to climb **354 steps** to reach the viewing area in the crown.

View from inside the crown

Hop on a ferry to New York City where BigFoot had fun in Times Square! (*BigFoot Visits the Big Cities of the World*)

GIFT TO AMERICA

The statue was a gift from the people of France, and was opened on **October 28, 1886.** Sculptor **Frederic Bartholdi** made the statue look like Libertas, the Roman goddess of liberty. Engineer **Gustave Eiffel** built the inside with iron to make the statue more stable. Eiffel would later build another famous landmark—the **Eiffel Tower** in Paris.

The tablet she carries has America's birthday (July 4, 1776) in Roman numerals.

The only way to get to Liberty Island is by boat.

Staten Island Ferry

The statue's nose is 4.5 feet (1.4 m) long, and her index finger is 8 feet (2.4 m) long!

GOLD TORCH

After the statue was cleaned and fixed up in the mid-1980s, a new **gold-plated torch** was put in place. The original one is on display in the monument's lobby. The statue was reopened to the public on its **100-year anniversary in 1986**.

New gold torch

GREEN LADY

The outside of the statue is covered with **copper**. It was originally **brown** in color. Over time, the copper turned **green**. This is what happens to copper when it isn't protected from the weather.

Original torch

Many believe the 7 rays on Lady Liberty's crown are for the 7 continents (Africa, Antarctica, Asia, Australia, Europe, North America, South America) and 7 oceans (Arctic, North Atlantic, South Atlantic, North Pacific, South Pacific, Indian, Antarctic).

1 BigFoot

1 Legendary Footprint

14 Red, White, and Blue Sailboats

17 Terrific Water Taxis

4 Wonderful White Cruise Ships

7 Soaring Seagulls

3 Floating White Blimps

5 Steady Staten Island Ferries

5 Peering Tourists with Red Caps

9 Hovering Helicopters

Notre Dame Cathedral

In the center of **Paris, France**, there is an island on the **Seine River** called Île de la Cité. The famous Notre Dame Cathedral is on the island's **southeastern edge**.

NEW BISHOP, NEW BUILDING

When **Maurice de Sully** was made the Roman Catholic Bishop of Paris in 1160, he ordered the building of a big, amazing cathedral. Construction began in **1163** and wasn't done until 1345. It was named Notre-Dame de Paris, which means "**Our Lady of Paris**," referring to Mary, the mother of Jesus.

BigFoot likes Paris and those yummy baguettes! Find him in *BigFoot Visits the Big Cities of the World.*

Napoleon Bonaparte was crowned emperor of France in the cathedral in 1804. He was a famous French ruler who conquered most of Europe.

A cathedral is a large Christian church that is the headquarters of a bishop.

MEASURING UP

Notre Dame is **427 feet** (130 m) long, 158 feet (48 m) wide, and **115 feet** (35 m) high. The towers are 226 feet (69 m) high. BigFoot will have to climb **387 steps** to get to the top of the towers.

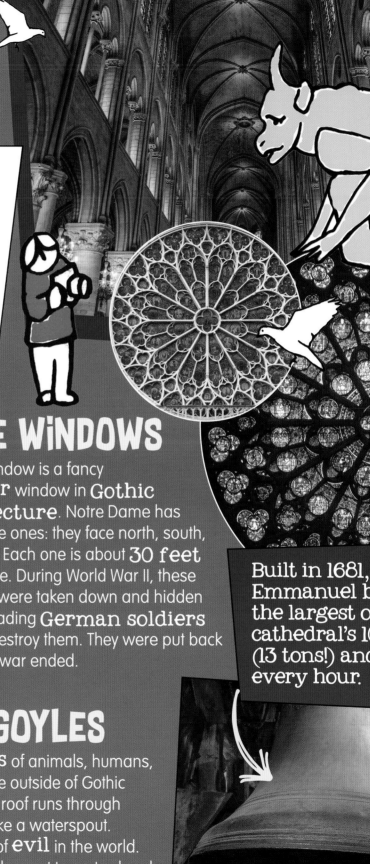

ARCHITECTURE

The cathedral's architectural style (how it looks) is **Gothic**. This was a new building style in the **Middle Ages**. Instead of the ceiling's weight resting on the walls, it rested on **buttresses** (supporting beams). The walls could then be thinner and taller. The cathedral is covered—inside and out—with tons of art: statues, carvings, paintings, and stained glass windows.

ROSE WINDOWS

A rose window is a fancy **circular** window in **Gothic architecture**. Notre Dame has three large ones: they face north, south, and west. Each one is about **30 feet** (10 m) wide. During World War II, these windows were taken down and hidden so the invading **German soldiers** couldn't destroy them. They were put back when the war ended.

Built in 1681, the Emmanuel bell is the largest of the cathedral's 10 bells (13 tons!) and rings every hour.

GRUESOME GARGOYLES

Gargoyles are **creepy statues** of animals, humans, or mythical creatures that are on the outside of Gothic buildings. **Rainwater** from the roof runs through the gargoyle and out of its mouth like a waterspout. **Gargoyles** were also symbols of **evil** in the world. They were supposed to make people want to go to church.

6 Perched Goat Gargoyles

9 Proud Parrot Gargoyles

7 Daring Dragon Gargoyles

7 Loveable Landing Pigeons

7 Red-Shirted Tourists with Cameras

Colosseum

AMAZING AMPHITHEATER

Emperor Vespasian ordered that the Colosseum be built in Rome, Italy, in 72 CE. It was finished in 80 CE. The huge **amphitheater** (a round, outside theater) was built with tons of stone and concrete. It sits on 5 acres (2 ha) of land and was 158 feet (48 m) tall. Around **50,000 people** could watch games, gladiator battles, animal hunts, and shows.

Below the Colosseum's floor were tunnels and rooms where the animals and gladiators lived.

COURTESY OF THE EMPEROR

When an **emperor** wanted to make people like him more, he would host a free event at the Colosseum. Sometimes there was even free food at these events.

The Colosseum is the largest amphitheater in the world!

ASSIGNED SEATS

People who went to the Colosseum couldn't just pick any seat: they were assigned by **Roman law**. The **Senators** sat in the best seats on the bottom level closest to the action. Behind them were lesser government officials, and higher up were Roman citizens and soldiers. The highest—and worst—seats were for servants and women.

TODAY'S COLOSSEUM

Much of the **Colosseum** is now missing or falling apart, due to years of vandalism, earthquakes, and fires. When earthquakes knocked down stones, they were used to build other buildings in **Rome**. But what is there now is still fascinating for thousands of tourists to see each year.

GLADIATORS

Gladiators were mostly prisoners of war and criminals who were forced to fight for **entertainment** in the Colosseum. At the end of a gladiator fight, the emperor sometimes let the crowd decide the future of a hurt gladiator. Many historians believe a **thumbs-up** gesture meant mercy, and a fist or **thumbs-down** meant death.

Gladiators who won enough battles to retire became celebrities!

1 BigFoot

1 Legendary
Footprint

7 Protective
Gladiator
Helmets

5 Loony
Lions

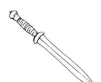
9 Super-Sharp Gladiator Swords

11 High-Flying Seagulls

6 Tourists with Blue Hats and Jackets

5 Curious Girls with Pink Dresses

6 Deflecting Gladiator Shields

Grand Canyon

LAY OF THE LAND

Located in **Arizona**, the Grand Canyon is **277 miles** (446 km) long. That's only 6 miles (10 km) shorter than the length of Pennsylvania, east to west! It's about a mile (1.6 km) deep, and is the **biggest canyon** in the United States!

The Grand Canyon was formed 5-6 million years ago.

GRAND CANYON NATIONAL PARK

NATIONAL PARK SERVICE

There are nearly 40 layers of rock that form the canyon's walls. These layers include granite, shale, sandstone, and limestone.

BiGFOOT
Goes On Vacation

BigFoot feels at home in national parks. He had a blast seeing Old Faithful at Yellowstone (*BigFoot Goes on Vacation*).

"The one great sight which every American should see."

—President Theodore Roosevelt, who made the Grand Canyon a national monument in 1908

SKYWALK

The Native American **Hualapai** tribe's reservation was established in **1883**. It includes part of the Grand Canyon and Colorado River. In 2007, the Hualapai tribe built a horseshoe-shaped, **glass-bottomed bridge** that goes out 70 feet (21 m) over the Grand Canyon. The bridge hangs 4,000 feet (1,219 m) above the bottom of the canyon. Hopefully BigFoot isn't scared of heights!

NEW FIELD OF GEOLOGY

Before the 1800s, most scientists believed the Earth was only a few thousand years old. They thought the shape of the land had been formed by **volcanoes** or **earthquakes**. Then in 1858, **John Newberry** studied the rock layers at the bottom of the Grand Canyon. He believed that the Colorado River had very slowly formed the canyon by **water erosion**, so the Earth must be millions of years old.

The first mule rides through the Grand Canyon were in 1887.

A canyon is a deep, narrow valley and usually has water running through it. The Colorado River runs through the Grand Canyon.

A geologist studies rocks and soil to learn about the history of the Earth.

Erosion is when the ground is worn down by wind, ice, or water.

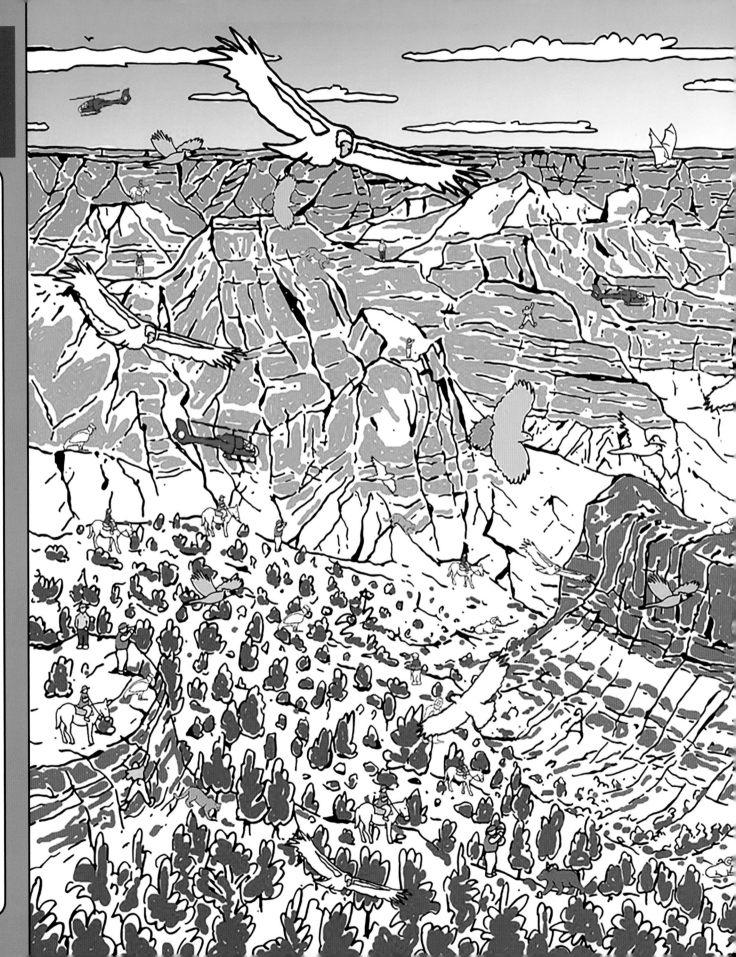

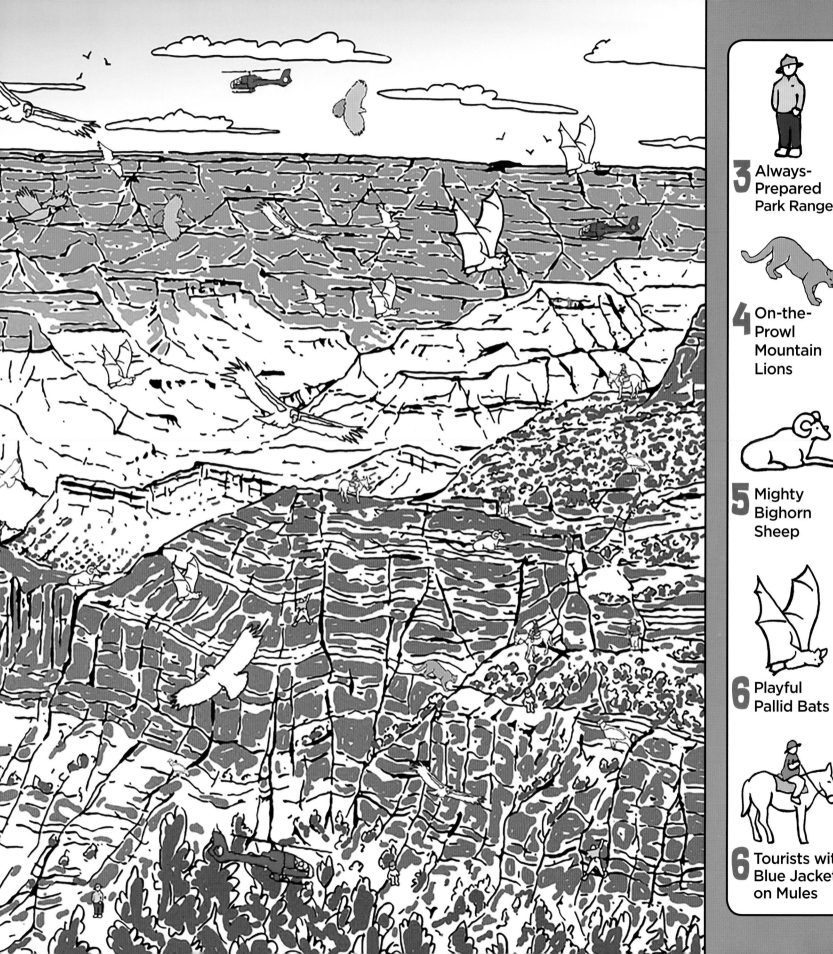

3 Always-Prepared Park Rangers

4 On-the-Prowl Mountain Lions

5 Mighty Bighorn Sheep

6 Playful Pallid Bats

6 Tourists with Blue Jackets on Mules

Uluru

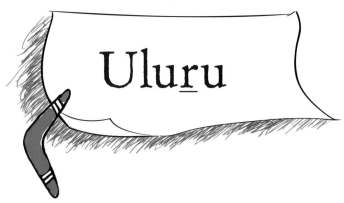

ROCK THAT WON'T ROLL

Uluru is in a national park called Uluru-Kata Tjuta National Park. It includes Uluru, a huge red rock, and Kata Tjuta, a group of large, domed rocks. Uluru rises from the flat Central **Australian desert**. It stands 1,142 feet (348 m) high. BigFoot will need to walk **5.8 miles** (9.4 km) to get the whole way around the base of Uluru.

LAND DOWN UNDER

Australia is "**down under**" the equator in the **southern hemisphere**. Summer happens between December and February. Winter is between June and August. This is the opposite of when they happen in the northern hemisphere.

Uluru is taller than the Eiffel Tower in Paris, France!

Dingoes are wild dogs that live in Australia. They don't bark—they howl!

RED BEAUTY

The best time to visit Uluru is during Australia's winter. In summer, the **temperature** can reach 116°F (47°C). The best time of day to see the rock is at sunrise or sunset. That's when the low sun brings out the amazing red color from the **iron** in the **sandstone**.

A boomerang is a curved club that is thrown overhand (like a baseball) and returns to the thrower. The world record for boomerang catches is 2,251!

A monolith is a large stone that is usually tall and narrow.

SACRED SPACE

Uluru is a holy place to the **Anangu**, an aboriginal tribe of people. An **aborigine** is someone who belongs to the group of people who originally lived in a place, unlike a group of people who came later. The Anangu have been living around Uluru for about 30,000 years. While the Anangu own Uluru and Kata Tjuta, they manage it with Parks Australia as a **national park**.

A wombat is a pudgy marsupial found in Australia. Babies ride in their mother's pouch until they're around 7 months old.

A group of kangaroos is called a mob.

Baby kangaroos are called joeys.

Kangaroos can go 35 mph (56 kph).

39

BiGFOOT
HEADS FOR ULURU

1 BigFoot

1 Legendary Footprint

9 Awesome Emus

11 Out-of-Control Boomerangs

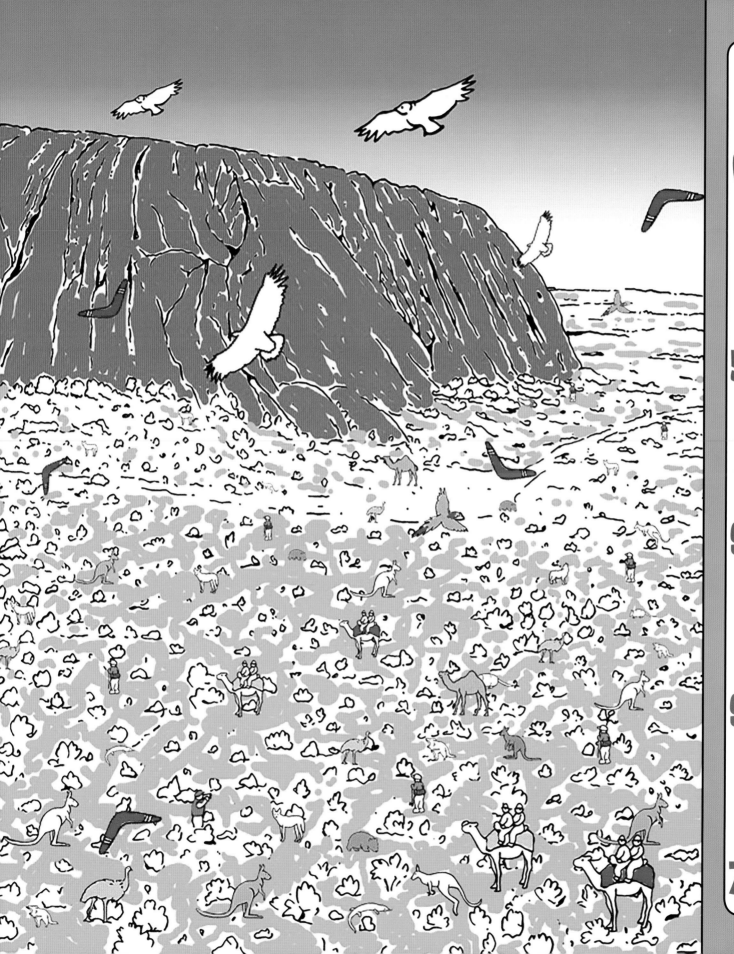

6 Brilliant Blue-Tongued Lizards

5 Kangaroos with Joeys

9 Delightful Dingoes

9 Dapper Dromedary Camels

7 Pudgy Wombats

Mount Rushmore

AMERICAN MONUMENT

Carved into the **granite** Black Hills of South Dakota are the faces of presidents George Washington, Thomas Jefferson, Theodore Roosevelt, and Abraham Lincoln on Mount Rushmore. This famous monument was designed by **Gutzon Borglum**. He began the project in **1927**. Work ended in October 1941, after Gutzon died and America became involved in World War II.

WHY THE LONG FACE?

Each president's face is around **60 feet** (18 m) long. On each face, the eyes are 11 feet (3 m) wide, the mouth is 18 feet (6 m) wide, and the nose is 20 feet (6 m) long. It took **400 workers** to sculpt the faces using dynamite, jack hammers, hand drills, and other tools. Over **450,000 tons of rock** were chiseled and blasted away from the hill to create this monument!

The mountain's name came from Charles Rushmore. He was a New York lawyer checking the gold claims there in 1885.

PRESIDENTIAL HEROES

These 4 presidents were picked because they did great things for America while in office.

George Washington: Father of the United States

Thomas Jefferson: Made the US bigger by buying the Louisiana Territory

Theodore Roosevelt: Helped US businesses grow and supported workers' rights

Abraham Lincoln: Led the country through the Civil War

HIDDEN ROOM

Gutzon Borglum dreamed of building a **fancy room** behind Lincoln's head to display historical American papers—a **Hall of Records**. A tunnel was blasted to start this project but then the dream ended. In 1939, Congress decided that work should focus on the faces instead. Then in 1998, Borglum's dream mostly came true. **Porcelain tablets** with text from documents like the Constitution were sealed in a vault in the unfinished Hall.

PLAN B

When the sculpting began, **Jefferson** was on the other side of Washington. After 18 months of working, the builders didn't like how it looked. They **blew up** what there was of Jefferson's face. Then they carved his face on the other side of Washington, where it is today!

Amazing animals you'll find at Mount Rushmore: Rocky Mountain goats, mule deer, bald eagles, coyotes, and marmots.

Scientists believe the shapes of these faces may last up to 7 million years!

1 BigFoot

1 Legendary Footprint

4 Bashful Bears

11 Mighty Mountain Goats

6 Orange-Jacket Hikers

4 Careful Climbers

11 Soaring Eagles

2 Wandering Coyotes

7 Busy Bird-Watchers

ANSWER KEY

Even at famous landmarks across the world, far from his home habitat, BigFoot is an expert at staying lost. He climbs roofs, hides behind buildings, blends into crowds—it's tricky work finding him! If you were stumped the first time around, you can use this guide—the **small red dot** shows where his elusive footprint is, while the **big red dot** in each picture reveals BigFoot himself. Just as in real life, the people, animals, and objects are easier to spot than finding BigFoot, so they are not included in this answer key.

BigFoot

Legendary Footprint

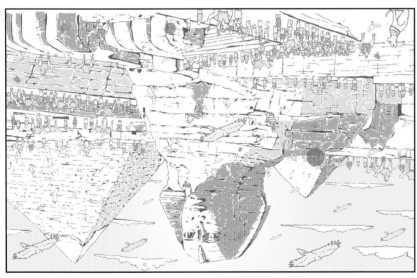

Pyramids of Giza

Golden Gate Bridge

Stonehenge

Great Wall of China

Statue of Liberty

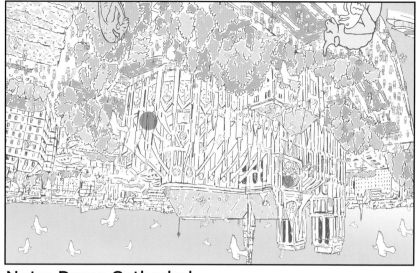

Notre Dame Cathedral

Colosseum

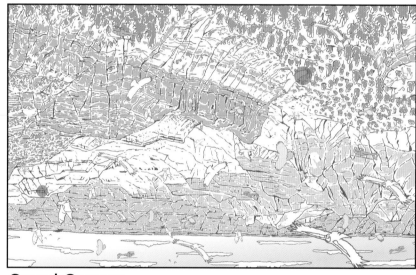

Grand Canyon

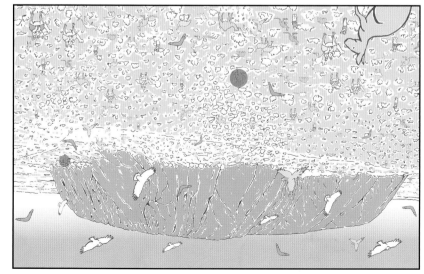

Uluru

Mount Rushmore

ABOUT THE ARTiST

As with BigFoot, the artist and creator of this series is a bit on the elusive side. He is rarely seen in public, spending most of his days sketching in his studio located among the mighty oak trees found only in the deep, dark woods far off the beaten path.

Deeply inspired by nature, the artist spent most of his childhood tracking creatures great and small across the rocky ridgelines and wooded mountainsides, perfecting his tracking skills and keen ability to spot what many of us never see. It was once said that the artist could identify approaching hummingbirds from two counties away with one eye, while tracking a fast-moving, bouncing black bear on a pogo stick with the other eye.

Despite his many accomplishments, his most important discovery and skill is the ability to spot the deceptive BigFoot that walks among us but remains unseen by most. After spending decades learning the habits of this elusive, mythical creature, the tracker/ artist has finally agreed to share his journals that capture the sightings of the infamous, larger-than-life creature that has mystified generations.

Now you have the opportunity to sharpen your search- and-find skills by finding not only BigFoot and his legendary footprint, but also the many other unusual and sometimes unexpected people, creatures, and objects that can be found at anytime . . . anywhere.

Happy Searching!